T0648377

Thank You

You

(a book for teachers)

sandy gingras

Andrews McMeel
PUBLISHING®

Andrews McMeel Publishing
a division of Andrews McMeel Universal
1130 Walnut Street, Kansas City, Missouri 64106

www.andrewsmcmeel.com
www.how-to-live.com

17 18 19 20 21 WKT 12 11 10 9 8

ISBN: 978-0-7407-9337-0

Library of Congress Control Number: 2009938768

ATTENTION: SCHOOLS AND BUSINESSES
Andrews McMeel books are available at quantity discounts with bulk purchase for educational, business, or sales promotional use. For information, please e-mail the Andrews McMeel Publishing Special Sales Department: specialsales@amuniversal.com.

Thank you
for believing in
me enough to

let me go on...

to discover more
Teachers

Student Story

"On the first day of English class, Mr. Bannon put a chair in the front of the room and propped a van Gogh painting on it. 'Look at this,' he told us, 'and write something so that I'll be able to see and experience this painting.' He honored us by giving us free creative rein and expecting us to be smart and interesting in the process."

Thank you for making mistakes...

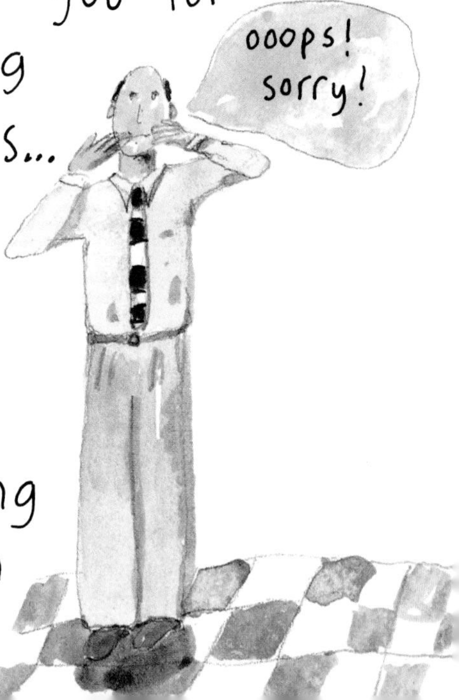

and admitting them

teaching me
to

Look and

See

teaching me
how to think
not
what to think

Sparking
me

stretching
me

letting me
discover it
myself

getting
it

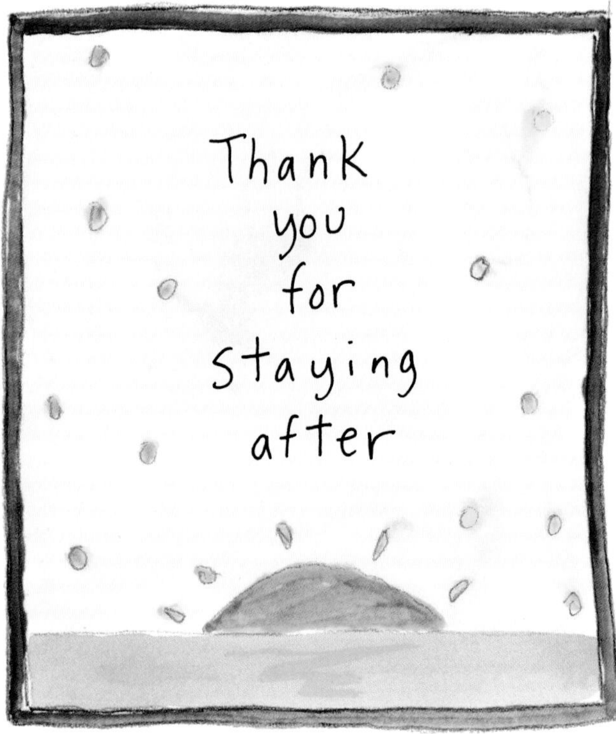
Thank you for staying after

being

a

noodge

Thank you

for
being
fair

BECAUSE...

"The greatest gift you can ever give is your honest self."

—Mr. Fred Rogers

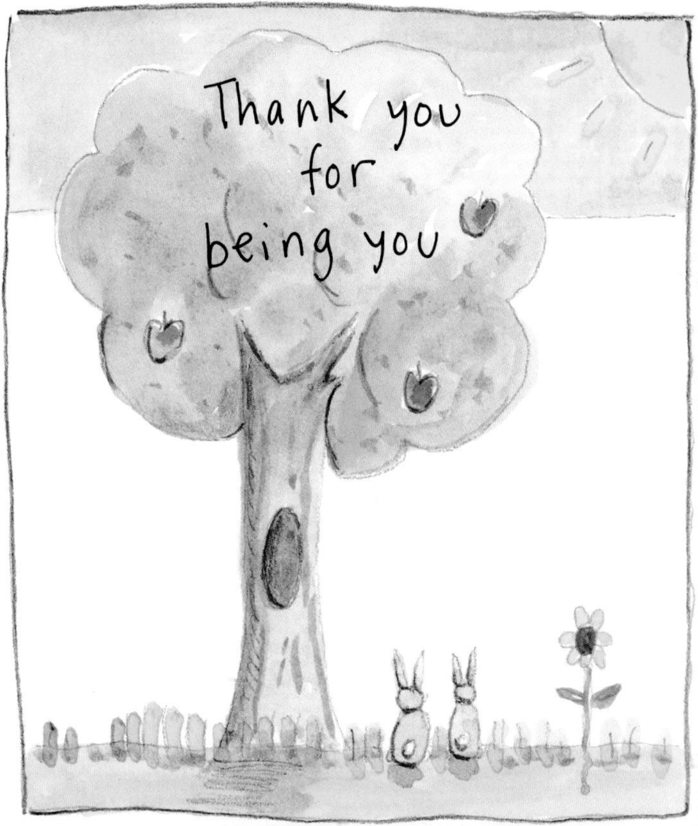
Thank you
for
being you

A life lesson:

"Politeness counts."

a tray of

birthday
cupcakes

Student Story

"Mr. Weishaus would have what he called 'collating duty' after school. For all the kids who, for whatever reason, didn't want to go home, this was a place to go—no questions asked. You could line up all the papers and neatly clip them together until the world seemed orderly again. Kind teachers like this, even in their quietest moments, help us make sense of our lives. They have a presence that speaks right to our hearts."

Thank you
for
Second chances

Words of Wisdom

"Do the best you can."

AHA!
momenTS

thank you
for making
me
practice

Student Story

"Mr. Miller was our golf teacher. He taught us to swing halfway when we wanted to swing full out. He taught us to take it quiet and easy when we wanted to play hard. It was frustrating, but he taught us about steadiness and consistency and showed us a new way to be strong. Sometimes you learn the most about philosophy when you're playing around in gym class."

thinking
outside

Student Story

"When we studied Egypt, Mr. Lorenzi asked us to make our own pyramids out of papier-mâché, then paint and decorate them. Then he hung each one on a string over our desks and told us, 'May the power of the pyramids be with you!' He was cool and creative, and our work became more powerful and interesting because of him."

Thank you for
seeing more
in
me

than I knew I had

teaching me
that slow and steady

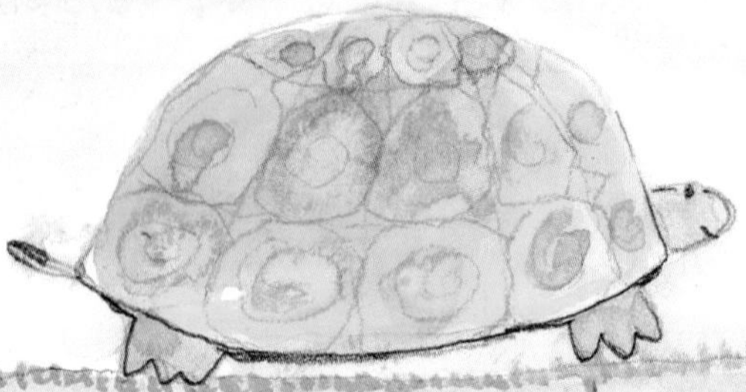

wins the race

rearranging
the
desks

pop
quizzes
(because life turns
out to be a lot
like taking the
test before you're
ready)

Lifelong Friends

Sam I Am
Curious George
Harriet the Spy
Huckleberry Finn
Jane Eyre
Harry Potter
Holden Caulfield

Thank you for knowing your stuff

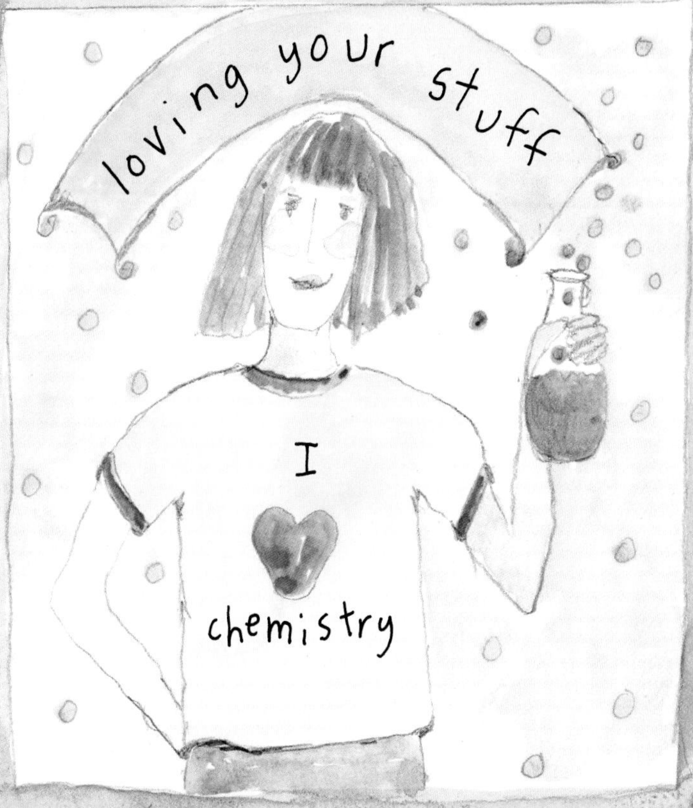
loving your stuff
I
chemistry

"The thing I remember best about successful people I've met all through the years is their obvious delight in what they're doing—and it seems to have very little to do with worldly success. They just love what they're doing, and they love it in front of others."

—Mr. Fred Rogers

Thank you for

making me
learn it
by
heart

Thank you for sending the bully to the office

the dreaded principal

Student Story

"Mrs. Plant took our third-grade class into the woods around the school at 8 a.m. every Monday. We were bleary-eyed kids, armed with a pair of binoculars and a field guide to the birds. We learned to identify birds, but mostly we learned to look and listen. You can't take away from a kid the sheer simplicity of a walk in the woods and learning how to be attuned to the fleeting singing moment."

reading aloud

Thank you for starting each day with a

clean blackboard

Student Story

"Mrs. Cook would clap her hands at our fifth-grade class and chirp, 'Isn't this fun!' with her wide-open freckly smile. We would all groan and roll our eyes, but her enthusiasm was contagious, and we got a little tickle-like giddy feeling every time we thought about learning."

gifts that endure.

Thank you

for...

best present is just to say,
"Thank you; I will remember
you; I will take you with
me on the rest of my
journey; I am better for
having known you."
   So this is a thank-you...
to all of the best teachers...
who do the hardest job
of all... and who give us

What can we give back to teachers for the gifts they've given us? How can we show them how much they've meant to our lives?

Well, the best present for a teacher is a life well lived. But the next

and to learn to
teach myself...

because
it's   the
process that
counts in...